Epic Cars

Mercedes AMG GT R

MEGAN COOLEY PETERSON

BLACK RABBIT BOOKS

Bolt is published by Black Rabbit Books
P.O. Box 3263, Mankato, Minnesota, 56002.
www.blackrabbitbooks.com

Jen Besel, editor; Grant Gould, designer;
Omay Ayres, photo researcher

Library of Congress Cataloging-in-Publication Data
Names: Peterson, Megan Cooley, author.
Title: Mercedes AMG GT R / by Megan Cooley Peterson.
Description: Mankato, Minnesota : Black Rabbit Books, 2021. | Series: Bolt. Epic cars | Includes bibliographical references and index. | Audience: Ages 8-12 | Audience: Grades 4-6 | Summary: "Experience what it's like to be behind the wheel of a Mercedes AMG GT R through exciting text, vibrant photography, and labeled images and other graphics"— Provided by publisher.
Identifiers: LCCN 2019028406 (print) | LCCN 2019028407 (ebook) | ISBN 9781623102579 (hardcover) | ISBN 9781644663530 (paperback) | ISBN 9781623103514 (ebook)
Subjects: LCSH: Mercedes automobiles—Juvenile literature.
Classification: LCC TL215.M4 P47 2021 (print) | LCC TL215.M4 (ebook) | DDC 629.222/2—dc23
LC record available at https://lccn.loc.gov/2019028406
LC ebook record available at https://lccn.loc.gov/2019028407

Printed in the United States. 4/20

Image Credits

mbusa.com: Mercedes-Benz USA, Cover (car), 6–7, 8–9, 10 (b), 14–15, 18–19, 20 (b), 27 (b); media.daimler.com: Daimler Global Media, 1, 3, 10 (t), 4–5, 16, 20–21 (bkgd & car), 23, 24, 26–27 (t), 28–29, 31; mercedes-benz.com: Mercedes-Benz, 12–13, 20 (t), 32; Shutterstock: Elenamiv, Cover (bkgd)

Contents

CHAPTER 1

Racing Down the Road

A Mercedes AMG GT R squeals around a corner. Its smooth body races by in a flash of color. Its strong engine growls, demanding people look.

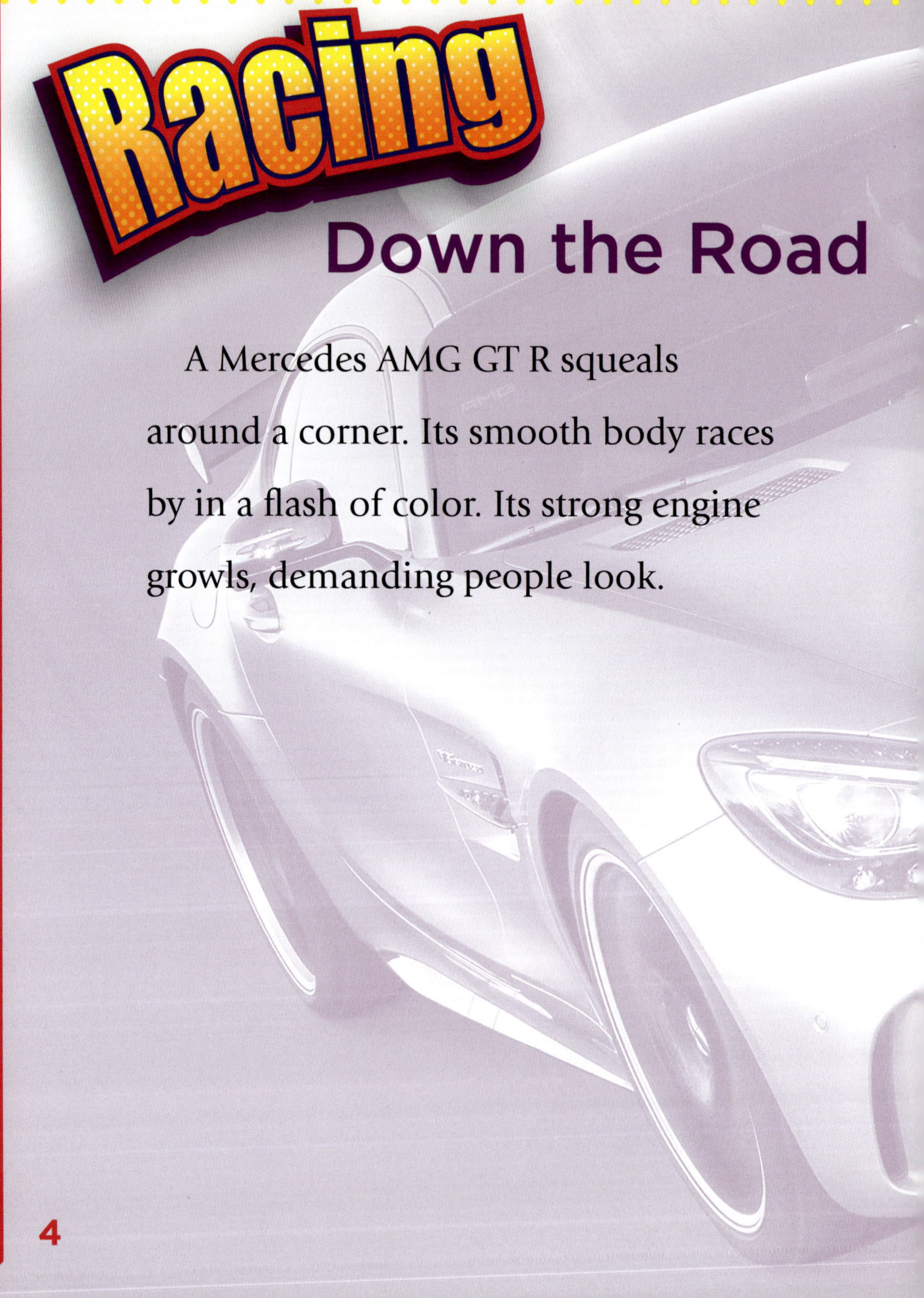

S GT 585

COMPARING HORSEPOWER

2019 Mercedes AMG GT R

2019 Acura NSX

2018 DBS Superleggera

2020 Audi R8

2019 BMW i8

Track Monster

The AMG GT R is one of the fastest road cars Mercedes has ever made. It zips from 0 to 60 miles (97 kilometers) per hour in 3.5 seconds. Some drivers also take it to the racetrack. At the track, it's called a track monster.

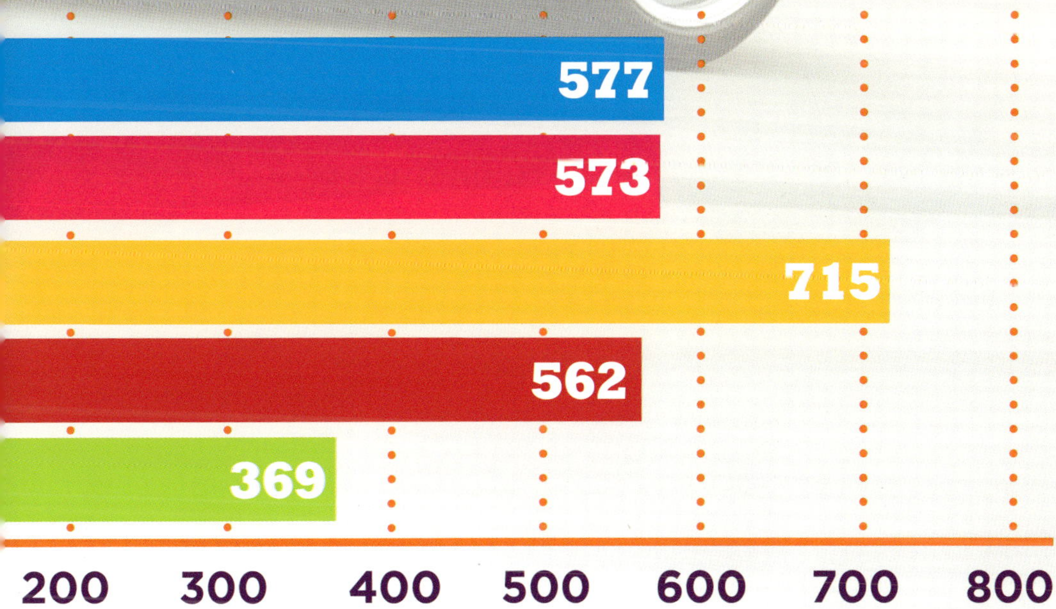

PARTS OF A MERCEDES AMG GT R

LONG FRONT END
GRILLE
SPLITTER

CHAPTER 2

Design

Mercedes designed the AMG GT R for speed. The car's frame is made of mostly aluminum. This material is lightweight. It is also strong and keeps drivers safe. A **carbon fiber** roof further reduces weight. Less weight allows a car to go faster.

The car's frame weighs only 514 pounds (233 kilograms).

The AMG GT R is made in Germany.

Grille

The car's black grille has 15 bars. Air flows through the grille and into the engine. This airflow keeps the engine cool.

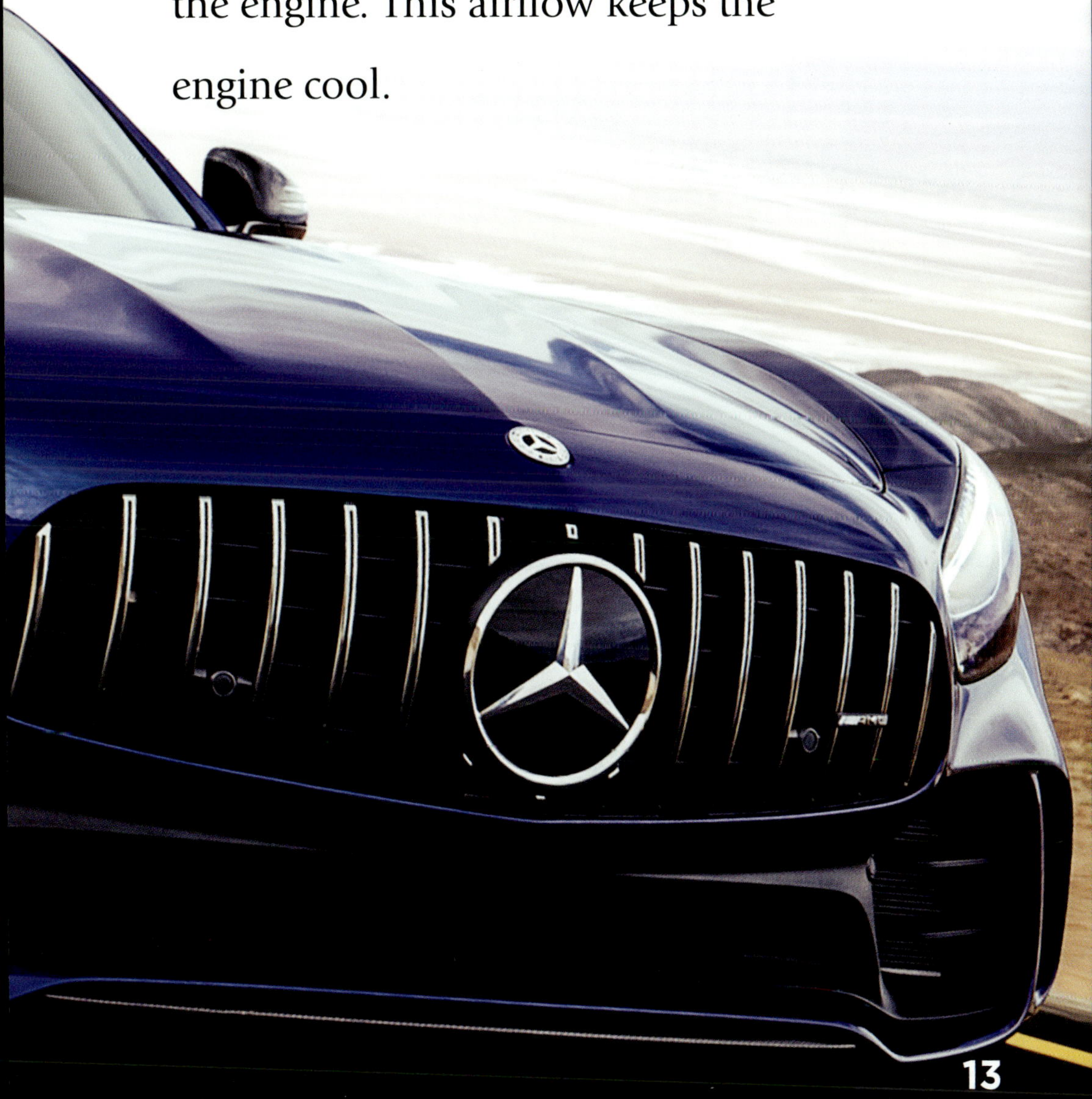

Aerodynamic

Engineers designed the car to be **aerodynamic**. Air flows easily over its smooth body. The rear spoiler and front splitter create **downforce**. At high speeds, downforce keeps the car on the ground.

V8 BITURBO

Interior

The race car experience continues in the car's interior. Racing-inspired seats have side **bolsters**. The bolsters keep drivers centered side-to-side. The center **console** has a shiny black finish. The AMG GT R seats two.

The AMG GT R has eight airbags.

Personalized

Buyers can personalize the AMG GT R to fit any style. They can choose from 12 paint colors. Inside, owners can even pick their seatbelt color. They can also choose carbon fiber trim on the doors, console, and dash vents.

AMG
MENU
SYNC
AUTO
RACE
ENGINE
START
STOP
P
R
N
D

AMG GT R DESIGN CHOICES

3
WHEEL OPTIONS

4
SEATBELT COLORS

12
PAINT COLORS

CHAPTER 3

Power and Performance

This Mercedes has an eight-cylinder engine. Each engine is hand built and signed by its builder. Twin **turbos** feed air to the engine, making it faster. The car can hit 198 miles (318 km) per hour. It drifts easily around corners.

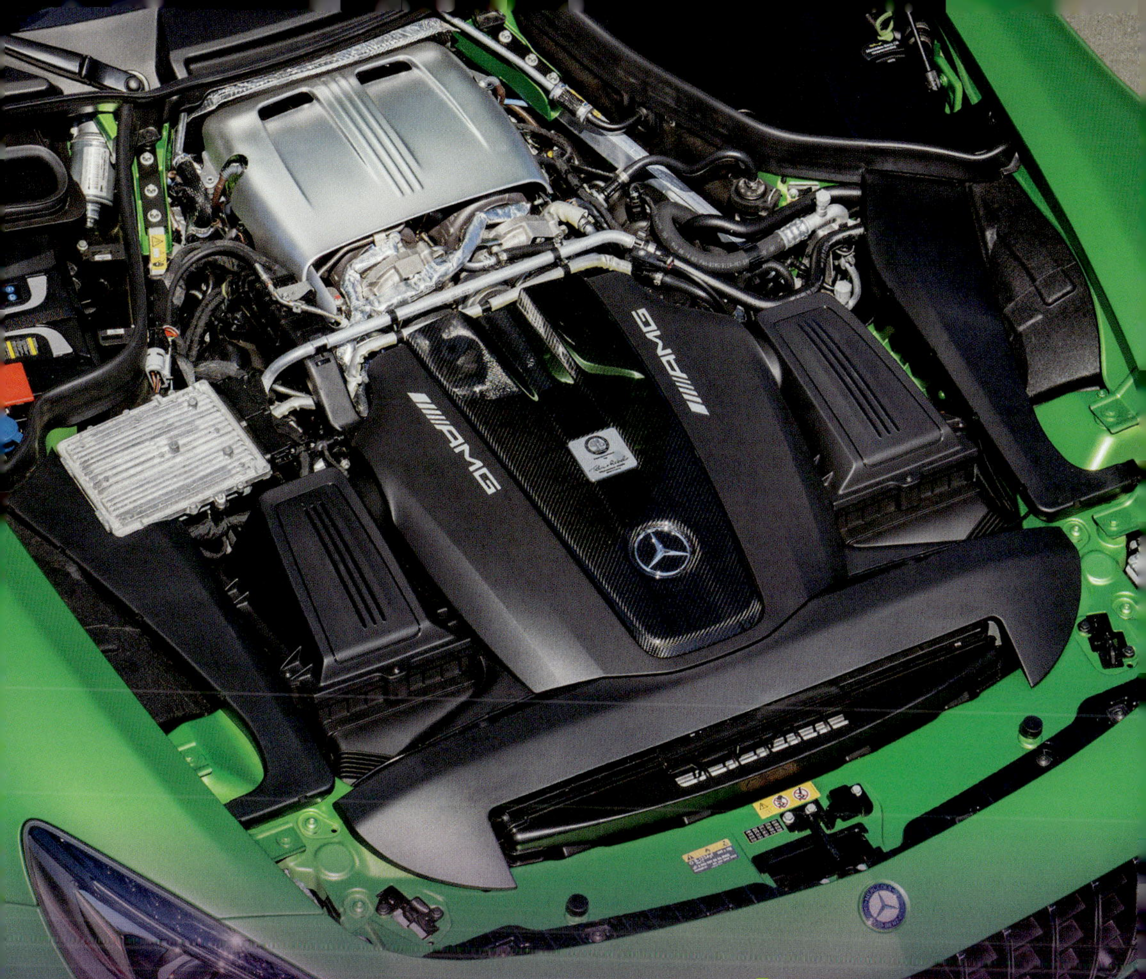
AMG
AMG

TOP SPEEDS

miles per hour
0
50
100
150
200
205 (330 KM)
198 (318 KM)
198 (318 KM)
191 (307 KM)
2020 Audi R8
2018 Porsche 911 GT3
2019 Mercedes AMG GT R
2019 Acura NSX

Drivers who like a loud roar can put the exhaust in loud mode.

A Fast Takeoff

The AMG GT R has driving modes. These modes change how the car handles. One mode is for everyday driving. In race mode, drivers can launch into a superfast takeoff. To launch, the driver presses the brake pedal. Then he or she pushes the **accelerator** to the floor. Once the brake is released, the car shoots off.

By the Numbers

179
INCHES
(455 CENTIMETERS)
LENGTH

81.7
INCHES
(208 CM)
WIDTH

50.6
INCHES (129 CM) HEIGHT

20
miles (32 km) per gallon

HIGHWAY GAS MILEAGE

$162,900

BASE PRICE
2020 AMG GT R COUPE

GB
190 MB

CHAPTER 4

An Epic Car

The AMG GT R pushes speed to its limit. This epic car leaves others behind on the racetrack. It also turns heads while driving down the road.

GLOSSARY

accelerator (ek-SEL-uh-ray-tor)—a device (such as a pedal) for controlling the speed of a motor vehicle engine

aerodynamic (air-oh-dahy-NAM-ik)—something that is shaped so it moves easily through air

bolster (BOWL-stur)—a long pillow or cushion

carbon fiber (KAR-buhn FAHY-bur)—a very strong, lightweight material

console (KAHN-sohl)—a small storage cabinet between seats in an automobile

downforce (doun-FAWRS)—a force that increases the stability of a motor vehicle by pressing it downward

exhaust (ig-ZOST)—the mixture of gases produced by an engine

turbo (TUR-bo)—a device that helps an engine increase power; turbo is short for turbocharger.

LEARN MORE

BOOKS

Bodensteiner, Peter. *Supercars*. Gearhead Garage. Mankato, MN: Black Rabbit Books, 2017.

Fishman, Jon M. *Cool Sports Cars*. Awesome Rides. Minneapolis: Lerner Publications, 2019.

Mason, Paul. *German Supercars: Porsche, Audi, Mercedes*. Supercars. New York: PowerKids Press, 2019.

WEBSITES

2019 Mercedes-AMG GT R
www.caranddriver.com/mercedes-amg/gt-r

GT R Coupe
www.mbusa.com/mercedes/vehicles/model/class-GT/model-GTR

INDEX